To
Siti Nonna

With all my love
Serena
xoxox

Hope it helps see you soon
love Jenna
xoxo

# How I Broke The Cycle...

*And why it took me 40 Years
to find the key*

by Teresa Lalloo

AuthorHouse™
1663 Liberty Drive
Bloomington, IN 47403
www.authorhouse.com
Phone: 1-800-839-8640

© 2010 Teresa Lalloo. All rights reserved.

Photography by Abbey of London Studios.

No part of this book may be reproduced, stored in a retrieval system, or transmitted by any means without the written permission of the author.

First published by AuthorHouse 7/8/2010

ISBN: 978-1-4520-4251-0 (sc)
ISBN: 978-1-4520-4252-7 (e)

Library of Congress Control Number: 2010909807

Printed in the United States of America
Bloomington, Indiana

This book is printed on acid-free paper.

THIS BOOK IS DEDICATED
TO MY DAUGHTERS

*To my heart and soul,
Monique and Jacqui.*

As you read this book, remember it was you both who inspired me to soul search back in time. It is because of you both that I stand strong today and every day of my life. For you both, I give my all. Know that, as long as God grants me the time with you both, there are no limits to my love for you. Ma will be there no matter what–till my dying day. I will pick you up and dust you off with kisses and hugs. You can do anything with God by your side, and I will always be your biggest fan. Don't let life pass you by, leaving you with regrets. Have a plan and believe in yourself. You were both planned by two, conceived by two, and loved by two. I hope our love has inspired you both to never settle for less. Remember that in order to build your lives–like a house–you need two things: the tools and a foundation. Those two things you have both been given, as well as the wings to fly!

This is your walk in the sand.

With all my love,
Ma
XOXOXOXOXOX

# How I Broke The Cycle...
## *And why it took me 40 Years to find the key*

**Chapters**

1. My Family – My World . . . . . . . . . . . . . . . . . . . . . 1
2. Could I Break The Cycle? . . . . . . . . . . . . . . . . . 13
3. Moving On . . . . . . . . . . . . . . . . . . . . . . . . . . . . . 27
4. The Truth . . . . . . . . . . . . . . . . . . . . . . . . . . . . . . 33
5. Too Much Too Soon . . . . . . . . . . . . . . . . . . . . . 35
6. Love Endures . . . . . . . . . . . . . . . . . . . . . . . . . . 49
7. Changing My Environment . . . . . . . . . . . . . . . . 55
8. My Happy Heart Breaks . . . . . . . . . . . . . . . . . . 61
9. What Happened / Losing Control . . . . . . . . . . . 67
10. It Began To Change Me . . . . . . . . . . . . . . . . . . 71
11. Breaking The Cycle . . . . . . . . . . . . . . . . . . . . . 77
12. Parting Words . . . . . . . . . . . . . . . . . . . . . . . . . . 79

---

A woman is the full circle.
Within her is the power to create,
nurture and transform.

~ Diane Mariechild ~

---

CHAPTER 1

# *My Family—My World*

On September 21, 1963, in the south Bronx, I was born to parents of Puerto Rican decent. I was not a planned birth; I was a mistake coming into this world. Mom and Dad lived in the heart of the ghetto–a rough and depressed area–and they already had one child they could barely afford. But even though I was unplanned, my mom always wanted me. That fact would never change, but the road ahead would be a hard one.

My mom had strong maternal instincts and a generous nature, but she suffered from a broken spirit. She grew up with alcoholic parents, and learned young to either hide or fight to save her sisters and brothers from beatings. Her parents were dysfunctional, and she was a product of that environment. She knew she was unloved and unappreciated as a woman; a curse destined to flow down the line generation after generation.

I was named after my grandma and was just six months old when she passed away, but for some strange reason I felt like I knew her. One day we were at Grandma's house, and Mom had me on a blanket on the floor. My grandma passed by me and I laughed to her. She turned to me and said, "Why are you laughing with me? Is it that you see the angels coming to get me?" My mom said, "Mommy, don't say that!" But Grandma just laughed as usual... she laughed at everything. When we got home that same day Mom got a phone call from the neighbor, who said a little while after we left my grandma had fallen to the kitchen floor. They called for an ambulance but by the time my mom made it to the hospital, Grandma had left us. She passed away from a brain aneurism. So, as early as infancy, it appeared I had a special gift.

Mom had just lost her mother, and now a second hardship was coming. Grandma had six children, three boys and three girls–of which Mom was the oldest. Although we lived in a one bedroom apartment, my mom's youngest brother and both of her sisters would be coming to live with us!

At the age of 22, Mom had the huge responsibility of taking care of three siblings as well as her own son and daughter. Unfortunately, she also had a husband who made life difficult.

She had an unsettled life with my dad who didn't know how to love, having never been taught that emotion himself. Ever since I could remember, my mom would cry herself to sleep, only to wake up in the morning as though life was OK. I can remember hurting at a young age *for* my mom–seeing her struggle through a hard life she hadn't bargained for.

Thanks to her, I never knew how poor we were. My brother and I were too young to understand the early problems our family faced. He was only two years old when Grandma died, but he was the apple of my father's eye–a fact well known.

Just like Mom, I grew up without the love and affection of my father, but she always filled in for the love Dad and I never shared, and for many years she succeeded in making me unaware of that loss. I will always be grateful that I was blessed with a mother so full of life and love–in spite of her own heartaches. She was able to share her love, attention, and understanding with us all, knowing it would take much work to raise a broken family. The oldest two children kept my mother's heart in turmoil, and the road ahead was bleak.

The eldest "child" of our newly reconstructed family was 13, my aunt (titi) Priscilla. She was angry at the world for taking away her mom and determined that the world would pay. To make our life harder, she disliked my dad (to put it nicely).

Next was my uncle Joey, only 10 when Grandma died. Also in great pain day after day over the loss of his mom. He dulled his pain through drugs which turned out to be a family curse that would follow us for years to come. He eventually became addicted to heroin. I recall my brother and I walking home from school and seeing my uncle and his drugged friends on the corner barely able to stand up. I was so embarrassed, but inside I loved my uncle and prayed that he would one day get better.

My aunt Nancy was only eight at time of her mother's death; very confused, but never giving my mom a hard time. She always held her own, and that would be the strength that helped her through a very difficult life ahead.

In the interim, who was loving my mom? I often wonder how she loved so deeply when she wasn't given love in return. The responsibilities that engulfed her made her set aside personal wants and needs, and move on despite deep inner pain. She concentrated on her children and poured her life and love into being the best mom she could be–with no reward in sight.

Her faith was her blessing; one I am grateful she passed down to me. As I grew up, Mom showed me the gift of church and the blessing of prayer and the wisdom of faith–of that she had a lot.

Even as a little girl I paid close attention to what was going on around me—sometimes a good thing, sometimes not so good. Fortunately for me, I was able to use my eyes to my advantage. My earliest observation that I remember is of Mom being a strong woman; she was careful to never let us see her down.

I remember my life around age four or five when we still lived in Hunts Point. We did the best we could as a family there in the south Bronx where there was no time to feel sorry for oneself and being soft was not an option. So I grew up to be strong. Tough. We weren't allowed to "rat," as my uncle would call it, on each other and if we cried we had better have a good reason or we would be given one. My father was never home, so mom was the acting head of house and she held faced life's challenges head-on. Never did I hear her complain.

Years passed. My Titi Priscilla was sent away with direction from our priest in our parish. She was only 16, but my mother knew she wouldn't be able to control her so she was sent away to a program in West Virginia for teenagers in need of direction. I can remember the day she left. I cried because my mom and my Titi Nancy were crying—not because I really understood their pain, but for my mother I cried. My mom was crying over her failure to keep her family together. It was the last request her mother had made of her, and she never forgot it.

My dad felt that with my Uncle Joey heading in the wrong direction, Joey needed to be enrolled into the military. He felt that it would teach him to be a man, as well as get him away from the neighborhood and away from his current "love." We were all being separated and I didn't understand why—only that my mom was always crying—so it wasn't a good thing. We stayed with my Titi Nancy who always loved me and set a good example.

My Titi Nancy's best friend Lucy was part of the reason my dad wanted my Uncle Joey to go on to the military. My dad was a man from the old school, to his convenience of course. With that said he felt that women's feelings are not important and must never get in the way of a male's path. But, all along, my Titi Lucy turned out to be the best thing that ever happened to Uncle Joey.

Even now, I can remember the pain of our family splitting apart like it was yesterday. Life at home wasn't getting better. My mom displayed a strong face to us kids as my dad tore her soul apart one day at a time. My dad was always a womanizer –claiming he was hunting with the boys or playing cards. And that is what I grew up believing, because my mom would never reveal my dad's infidelity to us. On the contrary, she always said, "That's your dad and you should love him for who he is." It was many years before I finally agreed with mom.

In the summer of 1972, my mother had finally had enough of the verbal and sometimes physical abuse, so she and Titi Nancy planned together for us to run away from home. My brother and I went to camp as we did every summer along with Titi Nancy who was a camp counselor. When it was time to leave one day, my brother and I noticed that we were going a different way home. When asked where we were going, Titi Nancy said, "Mom said to go to one of her friend's house and she will meet us over their to explain." I remember feeling scared of the unknown. Later on that night my mom sat us down and explained that she had chosen to remove us from what she felt was an unhealthy life. For me, somehow whatever my mom felt was OK with me, and still today it remains the same. The love and protection that my mom and my aunts provided for me was enough to last me a lifetime–and it has to this day. On the other hand, my brother was always very close to my dad and never understood our mom's choices when it came to Dad. There was always a division in our family, as if I was under my mom's and my aunts' protection but my brother was under my father's.

My Titi Nancy, God bless her soul, went through a lot with my mom, being able to recognize the abuse—even at her young age. This was a traumatizing situation for her and her best friend Lucy who later on turned out also to be my aunt, having married my Uncle Joey. "Thanks!" to both my aunts who spoiled me and sheltered me from the pain they recognized and endured; they were two of my protectors sent by God.

Eventually—and inevitably—my mom felt it was best for us to move back home with Dad. This time we moved into a two family home down by the water on Longfellow. It was a new start, or so we thought.

I later concluded this from the experience: A woman who has life throwing curve ball after curve ball at her, who has no education, and thus feels she has no choices, will almost always return to what she knows as 'normal'...even if she recognizes that 'normal' as dysfunctional. And then it usually gets worse. For us, it did.

One morning Titi Nancy woke us up whispering that my dad wanted us and my mother was in the hospital. "She's all right," she said. She was pale as a ghost but, as always, doing her best to buffer us from the distress and anxiety that she herself could not escape.

We got up to find our dad had gone crazy. Sitting in our front room, he cut up all my mom's clothes and threw them out the front window; the whole neighborhood could see that he'd gone berserk! Not only that, he took a hammer to my mom's wedding rings, while crying like a mad man. Dad sat my brother and I on his lap, and said, "Your mother left me." There was a song playing on the radio right then, and today when I hear it, I'm taken back to that place in time I would rather forget. On that day I don't remember feeling sorry for my dad. I was so worried that my mommy was OK.

Mom came home from the hospital to a life on Longfellow that was filled with ups and downs. Her dad came to stay with us. He was an alcoholic but, since most of my family was, that was normal for us. My grandpa took good care of us. Mommy finally started working and he helped her out by waking us up with hot cocoa or coffee and what seemed like a loaf of toast cut in half; one side was for each of us. He often took us on early morning walks, explaining, "The morning air is good for you." We walked down by the water where the prostitutes were. So naïve, we'd ask Grandpa, "Why are those women out here?" He would say, "They're working." And that was a good enough answer for us.

We had a lot of good times that stay present in my soul. My mothers' older brother Frankie (who we called Uncle Fafa) and his family would take us to Orchard Beach where we'd cook out, play with our cousins' swim toys, and enjoy a good old time. I loved family time! We had a big family with lots of cousins, aunts and uncles. We laughed together and cried together. But back at home, the interaction between my own mom and dad really didn't get better.

My mom was working, we were getting older, and life was running fairly smoothly for us. But just as we enjoyed some normalcy, my Nana died. Nana was my dad's mom. I had never seen him cry, and her passing was no exception. Two and a half years later my dad's father died, and two weeks after that my mom's father died. We were still too young to realize the void their passing left in our parents' lives.

The year that both grandfathers passed away we moved up to New Rochelle, New York, in Westchester County. It was a beautiful home; three stories with a yard, and we all had our own bedrooms. It felt like things were right. I was eight, my brother was ten; Titi Nancy was eighteen, and our lives seemed to be going in the right direction.

Titi Nancy was the first one in the family to go to college. My brother and I went to the catholic school down the hill. Mom went back to work part-time but was always home when we got home and had dinner ready by 3:00 p.m. My dad came and went as he pleased–like always–but we were content in our dysfunctional lifestyle behind the white picket fence.

We had more freedom in the suburbs. Our neighborhood was full of kids. My bother went fishing a lot, and he picked up several paper routes.

Mom took in foster children. It seemed that the presence of children in the house helped keep her from dwelling on her marital situation. She had several foster boys stay with us; some of whom I am still in contact with.

Years later when no children were left, Mom had a real hard time coping. It was the 'empty nest' syndrome, big-time. Without little ones to take her mind off her troubled marriage, and nothing to occupy herself, the disease of alcoholism (was it ingrained in our family's genes?) caught up with my mother. She began drinking to forget, but because of the alcoholism, she suffered even further because Dad preyed on her weakness by using her disease against her. He was good at attacking your weak spots.

She finally succumbed to a nervous breakdown, after years of play-acting that everything was as it should be while she ignored her husband's infidelity and his cold, detached nature. Dad broke her spirit once and for all. She went away, and later, we learned she had been placed in a mental ward.

My Titi Priscilla, grown now with kids of her own, was a strong woman in spite of her own troublesome life. She always stepped up to the plate when my mom needed her, so when mom needed her own 'time out,' Titi Priscilla moved in with us.

My dad's lifestyle wasn't affected. He continued to disappear on a regular basis.

It was during this time I discovered a suppressed pain of my own. I vividly remembered being molested by a man my parents trusted and whose wife I called my godmother. When it happened I had been very young... maybe five. Never had I shared this with anyone–not even myself until I was finally alone in my own room and able to hear my inner thoughts. When I did finally tell my mother, I found out that she too had been molested.

With all the pain my mom had been going through, I must have felt it best to hold on to that terrible invasion and store it until one day I might be able to share it. I had learned young to put things in their right perspective and move on.

Holding on to negativity would stop my growth and I had a lot to conquer. So as a youngster I kept a journal that seemingly worked to remove those entries from my memory bank, storing them on paper instead, and leaving me space for happier memories. I would not let others steal my joy; I learned to not carry pain. I instinctively knew those things would hold my soul hostage and not leave me enough strength to break the cycle. It was my solution to a sad situation, and it thickened my skin.

At the same time, I couldn't help missing the love my father showed my brother and not me. I didn't understand why he couldn't love me. I was a good girl and helped my mom out in the house. I had good grades. What did I do to make him not love me? Mom and I were very close and she tried to explain that although he loved me, he didn't know how to show me. That's when I realized that the *word* "love" was not enough for me. Just saying it wasn't the same as showing affection; I needed those actions that speak louder then words.

It was between the ages of eight and twelve when I figured out a lot and was able to build on my faith and know that I had to learn to love me for me.

I also began to wonder how my Mom's soul withstood all that coldness life dished her; why she stuck with her choice of husband–a man who couldn't learn to love or be loved. With my eyes now wide open, I started to think early about what I wanted for my own future.

I watched as my older brother worked hard and showed that he was not afraid to be different. At 13, he had three paper routes and shoveled snow in the neighborhood to make a dollar. He had a job to do come rain or shine and he kept his eyes focused. I thank him for leading by example.

I often heard my father say to my mom, "I got us out of the Bronx—what more do you want?" He was a man of few words and, when he did speak, he usually put his foot in his mouth. He came and went as he pleased. Later on we found out he had been living two lives and had two separate families. No wonder he always seemed to be withdrawn; he probably never knew which house he was in.

Maybe this was accepted by my mom, but I had a different idea on how I wanted my life with a husband to be. It was then that I began to take note of men around me and how they took care of their wives, and I wasn't impressed at all. It was clear to me what I *didn't* want in a man, and I thank God he kept my eyes wide open. I also saw the weak women who were so loving and accepting of their ill-behaved husbands. At the time, I thought it was a trait of just Spanish men.

Years later, after my brother had started college and I was graduating high school, my parents finally told us they were going their separate ways. I remember asking, *"What took you both so long?"* and that's when I found out that my mom had divorced my dad many years prior but thought it was best for us to have both parents around until we graduated high school! They had both agreed to stay and raise us together. It was the way marital strife seemed to be handled back in those days. My first emotion was anger at my mother for wasting so many years of peace and happiness for the sake of her children. But it was too late; at least the destructive years were finished.

Mom got better, but she needed to get out of that house where her illness was born. That meant leaving behind 20 years of all the hard work she put into our home. She told me, in order to save herself, the house was no longer important to her and that she now had to fight to keep her sanity. She just had to go. The rest of her family was upset at first with her leaving the house to my dad because they knew he would move right in with his new family. A small settlement was made, hardly worth the effort because it was a pittance compared to what she had put into making that house a home. But I began to realize that a house is not a home without love, peace and a healthy parents. Mom needed a clean break in order to get better.

So I had observed firsthand how a man can break down a woman when she feels insecure and her life is all about taking care of her children. Now I learned that someone could one day choose to move on and just leave you behind. If you were dependent on that someone, rather than feeling 100% able to take care of yourself, you would be left to flounder.

I admired Mom for what she had endured for our sakes, and for her courage during those years living with Dad, but I was determined not to find myself living a similar version of her life. I had to break the cycle.

For 20 years, my parents' relationship did not include love. It's hard to imagine merely existing in marriage for that long.

———————

Yesterday is history,
Tomorrow is a mystey,
Today is a gift...that's why
we call it the Present.

———————

CHAPTER 2

## *Could I Break the Cycle?*

I had always journaled, dreamed, and fantasized about what I wanted for my own life, and I knew there had to be a lot of changes coming. Get away; make a new start; break that cycle I grew up with. Those were some changes I'd need to make.

I got the chance for a new start when my parents and I moved up to New Rochelle. It was a pleasant and peaceful place to finish growing up. I saw green trees—not drug addicts on the corner. I could actually hear birds' chirping—not police and ambulance sirens. I liked it, and the change of pace allowed me time to dream. I felt like I was being lead to more important goals; I listened hard for the voice of my future, ready to follow.

My dad still had his own disgraceful agenda, but my mom always made the best of a bad situation, and that made life at our home fun. All the kids on our block wanted to hang out at 201 Coligni Avenue.

When we first moved, our neighborhood was predominately white; there weren't even many Spanish people in town. I had been an oddball at first but that changed, thank the Lord! New Rochelle soon became a melting pot with a mix of cultures and beliefs; close-knit, and without prejudices. We called our new location 'upper middle class.'

In my ninth year, on a Spring morning, a U-Haul® truck pulled up across the street. My girlfriend called to ask, "Did you see those boys that moved in across from you?" I looked out the window and to my surprise they were brown–like me. Another joy in my new world. I liked these boys, and they were from the Bronx. Three brothers; and they were so fine, all the girls on the block were picking which one they wanted! It was surprising, because we were all so young. What did we know about boys? But we were on the verge of finding out. And fate was about take control of my own little world.

Unbeknownst to me, God had heard my prayers and sent me my first blessing. Growing up I had always prayed, but I didn't ask for big dreams; only that my Heavenly Father would send me a good man. I didn't want to cry over a man's love like most of the women in our family had done. I'd seen them live it, and I didn't want it.

But back to the exciting new boys in the Lalloo family across the street: Hanif was 15, Ramon 13, and Wayne 10. For the next few years we bonded like brothers and sisters, playing from morning until the street lights went out and then I had to come in because I was a girl, but the guys could stayed out playing. I was always jealous because I wanted to be one of the boys; I'm still jealous of their gender-based perks. I liked the youngest brother, Wayne, but always knew he was too aggressive for me– we were too much alike. They called me a tomboy. There were only two girls on my block; the rest were boys, and we loved it.

Life was good. Summers, Mom or Titi Nancy would pile us in the car and take us to the community pool where we swam all day. Or, we would ride bikes, play at the lake, go to the local boys club for roller skating. There were also dances that I longed to go to. Alas, I wasn't allowed, since my dad was very strict with me. I was always much younger than the rest of the crew, but thought I was one of the boys and wanted to go everywhere they went. That just wasn't going to be possible with my dad's rules.

Over the course of the years our families became close. The three boys spent a lot of time at our house eating and hanging out, and me at their house. We shared our different cultures. I was Puerto Rican and they were Jamaican and I learned that they were a different breed of men. It was a breath of fresh air. We shared a lot of good times and some bad times, but all are great memories that I will cherish forever. Over time, they helped to restore my respect for men; they were gentlemen, and treated me with respect. They looked after me and taught me to never settle for less–a good lesson for my future.

Hanif, the oldest Lalloo son, was such a nurturing guy in that he always had my best interests at heart. I noticed little things like when he and I and the basketball walked down the street, he always walked on the streetside. One day I asked him why he did that he said it was the gentleman thing to do in case a car came towards us he would take the hit for me, and we laughed. That was just one of many things he taught me early on to expect from a man. It was funny how I soon became more worried about what Hanif would think than what my own dad's opinion was. My dad was hardly ever around, and even when he was he never really showed me any attention. Dad's focus was still on my brother Michael, who was the light of his life; and who could do no wrong.

Anyway, I knew by then that there was no sense being upset over the love Dad didn't show me. Remember, I'd been watching, and I never saw him able to love any woman the way I had imagined it should be. Yes, I *had* a dream to be loved by a man. At first, I had hoped that would be fatherly love from my dad, but it wasn't. I wanted a man to cherish me and my mother; even at age 12 this was very important to me.

Back then, I had no desire to become an educated and independent woman. My only dream was of falling in love and getting married–especially to a man who would be a loving father to my children. I guess you could say I was suffering from 'white picket fence syndrome' since that was what I called the way we were living in New Rochelle. You see, children from the Bronx didn't have houses. They just shared bedrooms and bathrooms; they didn't have a yard to play in. So to my way of thinking, *we had moved up big-time* and we now lived behind the 'white picket fence.'

Don't get me wrong, I had lots of fun in the Bronx. Our pool was the street's fire pump shooting out water with such force it would throw us! Playing in the park was great, despite the broken beer-bottle glass–and yes, we got cut. Although it was a rough and tough playground, in my family we were not allowed to be a 'punk,' as my uncle from Brooklyn used to say. But it did make us strong; thick-skinned, and *that* was going to come in handy for me!

But I loved our life in New Rochelle. I was happy the majority of the time, and when I wasn't, I had a way to deal with it. At night, I'd lay quietly in my bed building a relationship with my Heavenly Father. Mom always told me to pray when I felt lost or worried, unhappy, or simply needed guidance. So I used to pray. Mostly what He heard from me was: "Dear Lord, *Please* send me a man to love me for me." As I prayed, little did I know my husband was already with me all the time.

It had been nearly four years since the Lalloo family had moved into our neighborhood, and their presence continued to comfort me. We were all very good friends. Then one day I was outside when Hanif came home from school with a girl by his side. I felt a wave of heat wash over me, and I felt like I had to let off steam or blow my top. Later I did just that when Hanif came over–as he did almost every day. When he wanted me to ask my mom for a cigarette, I snapped, "No! Go buy your own." Puzzled, he asked, "What's wrong with you?" I said, "Why do you always bring girls home with you?" He said, "They're my friends, and they help me with my chores." I said, "*I'll* help you with your chores." He just stared at me until I said, "You *know* I like you." He said, "No, I did not. You're so young for me; your dad would kill me!!" Of course, he was right; he was five years older than me.

Weeks passed, and my little 12-year-old heart wouldn't stop pining for him. I was afraid to share my secret with my family because… what would they tell me?? Only that I knew nothing about love. They just wouldn't understand.

We often walked to and from school together. Hanif would walk me to my school then walk to his high school. And about three weeks after my jealous outburst, we finally kissed! A real kiss that sent chills up and down my spine! (As I write about this memory, I can still feel those chills today.) Hanif said, "We shouldn't have done that." He said, "I want you to know I like you a lot, but you're too young for me. I can get in trouble with your dad." I argued, "But my mom likes you a lot." "She wouldn't like it if I had sex with her baby girl though. And I'm at the age where I'm having sex, so that's one of the reasons I'm with those girls." I was crushed. In my mind, I screamed, *"No, you don't need them! …I'll give you what you need!"* But aloud, Hanif made it clear to me: "I don't want to have sex with you, you're way too young."

I was bursting with excitement and I had to tell someone. I remember running home that day, and telling my mom that I liked him and that we had kissed. Poor Mom—she held her head and said, "Your dad will kill us!" What I didn't know was—*she really meant it!* I bravely announced, "Mom, dad will just have to understand." She shook her head, and said, "No. He won't."

So began our strange relationship which continued for two years. We remained close as our love blossomed. He wouldn't touch me sexually, but his kisses were all I needed. It was a 'secret' that almost everyone knew, but nobody spoke about. I thought of him as my boyfriend—not realizing that Hanif was no different from the rest of the guys who had needs. After about two years, my brother (aka Inspector Gadget, aka my dad's spy) finally suspected and asked me outright, "Do you like Hanif?" I answered, "Yes" and brought down a load of trouble on myself. *Why did I do that!!!?*

Finally, my dad showed a sudden and *unsolicited* interest in me. He gave my mom a lot of grief over it, and he had my brother and all my uncles watching Hanif's and my every move. Suddenly, Dad had a lot to say. Next he made it his mission to destroy Hanif in any way possible. He told me he would put Hanif in jail. Then he called a family meeting and announced that Hanif was selling marijuana. As time passed, he became notorious for making loud statements to embarrass me—and he made my life miserable thinking that he could detour me from my dreams. But it was too late; God had sent me my soulmate (even if only I believed it was Hanif).

Over the next four years Hanif and I were not allowed to see each other. My dad made it Hell for both families. Remember, our families had been close—we were neighbors who lived right across the street from each other! So it was hard on us all—including our moms, whose efforts made it a little easier. Whenever they could, they began to make it possible for us to see each other. It seemed they believed in our love too.

It seemed like I stayed on punishment forever and, as always, Mom paid for it with me. Aside from my relentless yearning to be with Hanif, I was a good girl. I brought home good grades, studied Isshin-Ryu Karate, helped out at home and stayed out of trouble. But falling in love with a guy who was five years older *and of color*, really pushed my dad's buttons. Incredibly, he was prejudiced; I don't know why since he was a man of color himself. But he always used the N word loosely. I remember one day he came into the house and we were all sitting at the kitchen table as we usually did, watching mom cook. Dad said, "Jigger, jigger, a house full of niggers!" We all looked at him like he was a jerk–to put it nicely.

Our cat and mouse game went on; nobody was able to keep me from my first love, though my dad tried very hard., He had a way of brainwashing the men in my family. He had informed them that I was not to see Hanif–for any reason.

So one day Hanif and I were sitting on my front step talking when my uncle, drunk at the time, tried to load up a gun to shoot Hanif! I couldn't believe it...when he wasn't drinking, he was a fun and protective uncle. My dreams could have ended then and there; I knew my Heavenly Father was there by our side. While my uncle still fumbled with the gun, Hanif was the target, so he went home, but he was worried whether I would be safe. My cousin was there too and noticed that my uncle had the wrong size bullets, so we said, "Let's go to bed and things will calm down." We were scared to death but tried our best to fall asleep. We had almost drifted off when we heard someone coming up the stairs. We made believe we were sleeping when my uncle came in the room. He checked to see if we were in the bed, then walked out. *We were so scared!!* This was just one of many crazy antics that I lived through during those four years. I was beat, slapped, and punished–allowed out only with my mom.

During those years I viewed my dad's actions as those of a ruthless man who saw life as his private game–but he cared nothing about the other players. And now I was smack in the middle of the game. (A long time later, I forgave Dad. There is power in forgiveness and I needed to set that part of my soul free. It was part of taking care of ME.)

Because of all she had to endure under Dad's roof, my mom finally turned to drink, and eventually the curse of alcoholism would fall upon her.

I was so happy to have my own room…a solitary comfort zone where I could shut out the craziness and focus on things–like music–and soul-searching.

When I was about 13, Titi Nancy was one of my greatest mentors. I could talk to her about all kinds of things. She often took me shopping at a clothing store where she worked; that always made me feel better. She also paid for me to attend a karate school her friend owned. She said it would keep me focused and let me release some inner anger. This turned out to be a very helpful tool–and I learned to love karate. I also learned that the mind controls the body, and we are in control of our mind, body and soul. I went to karate for 3 years, had the opportunity to enter tournaments–and even won many. I learned to focus on my strengths and to build tolerance by running, exercising and stretching. This is where I learned structure and confidence. Thank you Titi Nancy for helping me develop my assurance!

Nancy was my Mom's baby sister, and I looked up to her. She was also the first one in our family to break many cycles. My Titi Nan was beautiful both inside and out, but I knew there was even more to her. I saw a woman who wanted more and who worked hard to get it. My aunts have always promised that if I ever needed anything they would be right by my side, and they were. As a teenager, you *always* needed something. Every little thing was such a big deal, but I had three marvelous aunts who were always there to listen and never to judge. It was so easy to open up to them. Even to this day, their example has helped me to be that same type of mentor to teenagers around me.

But though I was thus saved from a lot of teenage angst, my tender heart still endured a lot of misery. I spent too much time at the window watching Hanif and his brothers hanging out, bringing girls home. I stayed up all night sometimes just to see what time they left. Love made me crazy.

Many times I would hear comments like, "Teresa, don't you know Hanif must be seeing other girls?" or "Well, sure, he's probably still having sex, don't you think?" Even worse were stories of people seeing him out socially with girls. The thought of someone other than me being out in public with Hanif twisted my heart. I knew he was popular, but I waited. And suffered. It was a long four years.

Thank God for my mom! We suffered together.

One day in gym class we had swimming and I was in the pool talking to one of my classmates about her cousin dating a black boy. They were Italian, and the girl's cousin was keeping the relationship a secret. I was particularly interested because I had the same secret relationship problem. She went on about what a nice guy he was and how he wasn't really black–he was Jamaican! When I asked his name and she answered, "Hanif," I thought I would die. My heart pounding, I slowly backed away from her and out of the pool.

When I got home, I called Hanif and asked him if he knew who Nina was. Of course he said, "No." It took days of doing my research to find out more than any young girl would like to know. She didn't even speak English!

I had put Hanif on a pedestal. He was supposed to be *my soulmate!* I wasn't yet 14, and already I was in love–and in agony because of it. My love was older, and still out there as a player–when I was a 'child' who was "not allowed" to play. This just broke me into pieces. As always, my mom comforted me, as I did her. She warned, "This is the first, but it won't be the last." and then consoled with, "This, too, will pass." But I thought, "No way, Mom–this pain will *never* go away."

But Hanif did own up to all I had discovered, and displayed sympathy and concern for my feelings. Most of all, he made it clear to others that although we weren't able to see each other he loved me and no one could take that away from us. Not that it mattered to other girls; I soon learned that others always want what they cannot have. Hanif soon stopped seeing Nina, but Mom was correct that she would not be the last. I dealt with this until I was 16.

Against his will, and most likely thinking it would never happen, my father had told me, "If you still feel this way at 16, I'll allow you to start dating him." The year I turned 16, my parents gave me a traditional sweet 16 party–very meaningful in the Spanish culture. And Hanif was allowed to escort me! I couldn't have been anymore excited.

Over the past years we had been through a lot of ups and downs–always growing deeper in love. I turned 16 when Hanif was 21. He was a well-rounded man; a man who loved his mother, and that meant a lot to me. My mom always told me to watch and see how a man loves and respects him mom and that would give you a good indication of the man he will turn out to be. (Right again, Mom!)

My mom loved Hanif and believed in our love; that was so important to me. She taught me no one is perfect, but that only I could decide what imperfections would be acceptable to me.

I haven't mentioned Hanif's dad. He was a quiet man until he drank; and then he turned into another person. He was a loving dad to his children until they grew up and could think on their own. Then he checked out of the relationship and started showing other colors. Hanif's mom was a strong and intelligent woman who held back no punches and I loved her for that. But her children were growing up fast, and she had to devote herself to her own agenda. So his parents were going to divorce.

I had learned a lot watching women. Some stood strong even though their lives were a constant battlefield. Some suffered as though in prison and never escaped. Some took steps to secure their futures, and some to happily raising children on their own. All this prepared me for choices I would have to make–and sooner than I thought. But as for my true love, I had long ago decided what I wanted. It was right by my side.

Time went on, and I was falling deeper in love with Hanif as both our home lives were falling apart around us. Even as a young man, I felt that Hanif stood strong and there would be no reason for me to worry about his character. His inner strength felt so good to my soul.

On a Saturday, Hanif and I were walking through the mall, and as we walked we passed a jewelry store and he stopped me at the window and asked me if I liked the ring behind the glass. *It was a diamond ring! ...and it called my name!!* I wasn't certain where he was going with this, but–as always–he lead, and I followed. So, we went in to try it on; oh my, it fit me like a glove. He asked me if I wanted it. I remember looking at him with my heart almost beating out of my chest. I answered, "Yeah, I want it; but can we afford it?" But by now I knew Hanif could make just about anything possible, and he went inside and asked if he could put our ring on layaway. After that day we never spoke about it much, but the anticipation of being engaged bubbled just below the surface. And to speed up the process, we *both* made payments on the ring depending who got paid that week.

Around this time, Hanif's parents' divorce became final and his mother moved herself and her sons to the next town that we called "money-earnin' Mount Vernon"! She had her own apartment, and the three boys were in a second apartment in the same building. I was now 17, soon to be a Senior in high school. I decided to move to Mount Vernon and live with Hanif and his brothers until he and I could get our own apartment. Then I would get a good job and start my life.

Hanif and I were getting ready to go out one day–pretending to save water by showering together–when he silently reached out to the medicine cabinet. When he pulled his hand back in it was holding 'the ring.' *I was stunned.* He had totally surprised me; I thought we were still making payments on it! Under the showerhead, he just slipped the ring on my finger, and never did officially ask me to marry him. 27 years later, he still jokes that he never really proposed. And, to be truthful, I *was* the one who just moved right in!

Planning my wedding made me very happy. My home life had been so 'grey,' but *this* was a rainbow! My very special Aunt Nancy gave me a lot of guidance, leading by example. She was moving in with her fiance, a long time boyfriend, and they would soon be married. My uncle-to-be, Brian, was a solid man and while I was happy she had found a man of meaning, I was very sad to see my childhood home emptying.

High School Graduation was right around the corner, and our wedding date had been set for July 17, 1982. It was a time of sad parting, in the midst of blissful expectations for my future. It was a bittersweet passage. And it was during this turmoil in my life that Mom threw her own world into a spin, leaving home with only the clothes on her back. She wanted no souvenirs from her marriage to my father. He barely came home anyway and our house was no longer a home.

Mom moved back to the Bronx, and my brother was away at college. Aunt Nancy was marrying ...and I was really just starting to mature, having been kept so sheltered at home from age 12 through 16. I was virtually a little girl suddenly living in a woman's world. But living together was good; it gave us time to know each other on a whole new level. They say you don't know someone until you live with them? Well that's the bare truth! During this time we fought hard and loved hard. But I never doubted that I was where I wanted to be, so at the end of the day I was still in my comfort zone.

I would often go down to visit my mother; we remained very close. She always supported my journey, and I will always be grateful for her unconditional love. As I started a life of my own, she had nothing but love for me. At the time she was suffering from empty nest syndrome, but I was too wrapped up in my new life to notice. She was drowning in pain, and she continued drinking to mask it. She had never burdened her children with her pain and this fight, too, she'd take on by herself.

I knew she wanted more from me, but I was just beginning to find my own way. I had to concentrate on keeping myself on the path that I had chosen. I needed to be sure that I broke that cycle–I simply had to move forward.

_____

If you believe it and see it—
whatever it is—
it's within your reach.

_____

CHAPTER 3

# *Moving On...*

In June of '82, I graduated from New Rochelle High School, and was to be married the next month on July 17. I was 18.

From an emotional standpoint, leaving home wasn't typical for me. Most daughters grow up with the first man to show them love and affection being their father. And then, later in life, affection wouldn't be the number one all-consuming quality she would look for in a man.

Thankfully I had been sent a loving man to marry who would also be a help to guide me every step of the way. I loved and respected Hanif as much as I would respect a father. As a matter of fact, my new nickname for Hanif was "Papi."

Dad never did accept Hanif's and my choice to marry so young. And that was irrational, because... what other choices did he ever give me? I don't remember him ever asking me if I'd like to go to college, or giving me the moral or financial support to pursue anything more.

And my dad made one other part of our wedding difficult for me... he insisted that his second wife attend. What I haven't mentioned to this point is that he had been with this woman for 20 years, and she was 'the other woman' in his marriage to my mother during *my entire life!* She was as betraying as Dad, because Mom had befriended her for many years. Having her at my wedding did not sit well with the family; but, my gracious mother told me to follow my heart. She said that it was my special day and she wasn't going to take that away from Hanif and I; and so my father's wife was included. My mom was always so unselfish.

Hanif and I spent a lot of time talking about plans for after our wedding. We needed an apartment of our own. We had no furniture to put in it, but I didn't care. With the love and protection that my Papi provided, I could be happy anywhere. We had already been living together for about six months, which gave us time to discover our differences—and there were many. We were complete opposites in every stretch of the imagination. At times it was difficult, but never frightening; this man made me feel safe and grounded. You see, Hanif is a calm man while I am a wildflower.

When July 17 arrived, it was scorching hot! That afternoon, in Holy Family Church, Hanif and I were finally joined as husband and wife. Everything was just as I had dreamed it would be.

My mom was so happy. Her prayers that I *not* live the same life that she had were being answered. God is good. Hanif and I shared the day that everyone said would never come with all our family and friends. We were blessed with each other, and our union was strong.

That night we invited everyone to Hanif's old apartment and partied until *6:00 am!* Then Hanif and I went to a local hotel. We spent the next day in our room, luxuriating in the fact that we were finally man and wife; also rejuvenating and preparing ourselves for our honeymoon trip.

The next morning we headed to the airport. *"Hawaii, here we come!"* On the way, I remember being thankful that I had not given up on my dream. I had done a lot of growing while planning a wedding, getting an apartment lined up, graduating one month and marrying the next. It was quite a roller coaster, but the payoff was so worth it: My long-time dream of marrying Hanif was realized. And now, honeymooning in beautiful *Hawaii!* Five days of fantasy with the love of my life. It was all that I imagined... the sights, the smells, the island of paradise. It was a trip we vowed to repeat, and we did later–with our children.

Also in Hawaii, there was family that I hadn't seen in years. I couldn't wait to see my Uncle James, aka Chicky. He was my mom's most troubled brother, so mom had sent him to live with my Uncle Frankie (the oldest of the six) and there Uncle Chicky stayed until he passed away–much too young. Growing up, he was always fun and made us laugh until we had stomachaches and couldn't breathe. We were both so happy to see him.

Coming home was good as well. I had missed my mom and had so much to share about our family in Hawaii and how good they were to us and how much we laughed. Yes, some things never change; my Uncle Chicky still considered life his playground and he loved the rides.

When we came back we moved into our own studio apartment at the Park Avenue in Mount Vernon where Hanif's whole family lived. I wasn't joking about the furnishings...it was bare except for a couch that Hanif's aunt had left us, and that was our bed. One couch...but we couldn't have been any happier. The family partied every weekend, and we had a good time with hardly any money in our pockets. But the rent was always paid and we were employed, so life was good. We had very little money and that taught me to work hard. I had worked in the bank part-time while in high school but now it was time to get a full time job with health benefits.

I had landed a good job with a real estate company in New Rochelle. I ran for that 8:05 a.m. train everyday. We had a young vibrant boss that taught us to work hard and play hard. He often took us on his yacht and to Manhattan where we learned to love the Broadway plays. It was by far my happiest job, and there I stayed for the next six years. I worked hard, but enjoyed new exciting lifestyles, and grew in so many ways. It's because of those days that I love Broadway and the Big Apple...a.k.a. The Concrete Jungle!

Hanif and I took time to plan a family. I wanted my life to be solid when we brought children into the world. So for the next three years we worked hard; but, boy, did we play hard too. We were young, and hanging out until the sun came up was normal for our crowd. I guess we needed to get that out of our system in the first years of our marriage. We had two salaries, but sometimes only had enough money to pay the rent and buy our train passes for the next two weeks to get us back and forth. We had no car, but we knew we would eventually save to get one.

Soon after our wedding, my friends went off to college and wanted me to come hang out with them, but it wasn't often I could make that happen. You see, I now had an obligation to being the best wife I could be. This was very important to me; in the Spanish culture, being a good wife was like achieving a college degree. (Sad, but true.) Hanif was also somewhat old fashioned. His culture was the same as mine in many ways–in that a married woman had her place, and it *wasn't* out in a bar with single friends. The family he grew up with believed this.

Yes, I was totally fulfilling the dream of my youth, but as a maturing young woman, I could see that "breaking the cycle" meant more than loving and marrying a good man. Love could still make you a prisoner! *"A married woman had her place?"* Not this woman! Now it was about *me* as an individual being able to make my own choices and feeling 100% in control of my own life. Remember, for the past nine years Hanif had called all the shots, and I had encouraged this.

Now, after many years, I realized that I had not yet reached my objective. I did not feel confident and in control of myself and my happiness. Before Hanif and I started a family, I needed to make clear to him my views on self love. My goal was to feel 100% complete at the end of every day–with or without the help of anyone or anything. I had watched the women around me living their lives…so dependent within their marriage. I was not going to be one of those women.

While Hanif already knew how important this concept was to me, he was just finding out that, as my husband, *he* would also be feeling the effects of my "breaking the cycle." If our marriage was to last, I would have to always be 100% true to myself, and it would not be easy.

———————————

Life gave you lemons?
Make lemonade!

———————————

## CHAPTER 4
## *The Truth*

The truth is, my Heavenly Father had heard me. He had sent me a one in a million type of man just as I had asked Him. The truth is, the odds were against us; most people viewed what we had as a crazy puppy love. But I felt I had hit the lotto.

The truth is, I wanted our marriage to work more like an equal partnership. I wanted my soulmate to be equal and fair with me–not like the old school, where women should be seen and not heard. So my mission was to make ours a "give and take" marriage. One where we were both necessary, but also both unrestricted–free to operate as individuals. Functioning at 100% each meant we'd have a 200% union–twice the chance at a long term marriage!

I came from a family whose joke was that the man was the king of his castle. But in *my* world, there was only one King and that was my Heavenly Father. He had given me life. Now He was watching to see what I would do with that gift and how I would respect and improve my journey. I needed to make that clear to Hanif.

I always wondered when I heard women say that their husbands "made them" do something. I silently wondered, "How can someone *make* you do something you don't want to do?" This question was ever present in my mind as I became a wife. Hanif soon came to realize that I was a strong and outspoken woman who had a mind of her own. I found it difficult to hold back who I was. I noticed that I had gotten something good from my dad after all... his strength–but both his good and bad–and I had to pay close attention to only nurture the good. Hanif was passive and non-confrontational, and I was aggressive, wanting to be in control. So we learned early on that we must 'agree to disagree' to make our journey together a healthy and happy one.

Life has taught me that men don't take well to women who are strong willed. We're labeled 'bitches.' Well, that was a label I was willing to wear, if it meant being a woman of leadership. In that case, I'd own it!

The *truth* was, after nine years, life behind the white picket fence was nowhere near what I wanted for my reality. I wanted more for me. I wanted this one life of mine to carry equal weight in our marriage. I wanted to know that my opinion was important to the man I had chosen to take this journey with.

Little girls learn that growing up, falling in love, living behind a white picket fence, and being a good wife and mother, is "the perfect life." What an overly romanticized version of life!

A big stretch from *The Truth* as I saw it.

CHAPTER 5

## *Too Much Too Soon*

When I turned 22, Hanif and I were still working hard and living in a nice little studio apartment. We had already applied for a two bedroom, and were ready to stop the constant partying and start a family. I still worked for the real estate company that managed over 100 buildings in the tri-state area.

We felt we had a good life, and a foundation built, so it was time to try for a baby. We were the first in our circle for everything, and now we would have a baby. I was so excited; I had such a burning desire to be a mom. Every month I thought I would be pregnant. It was a joke with my family and friends. Months passed, and no baby. I thought sex with no protection meant you were supposed to get pregnant! Not the case since I'd been on birth control for so long. After six months, I was really impatient, but I finally missed a period. After another month passed, I bought a maternity blouse, wore it to work and told everyone I was having a baby. The next day I got my period. I cried for days, *and* I had to tell everyone I wasn't having a baby after all. Two more months dragged by, and then one day I felt sick at work in the morning. Hanif bought us a test that came out positive. Joy! Finally our dreams of having a baby were coming true and Hanif and I couldn't have been happier.

I had some sickness for the first three months but Hanif was always there to take care of me. And I had constant support from my mom and my aunties–growing stronger every day. Even though I was now going to be a mommy, I was still a spoiled brat (and that never has changed!). It was a happy nine months; everyone at my job brought me food–lots of fruits, or anything I wanted. I remember that I loved sugar Frosted Flakes® and I usually brought some to work with me. One day I got to work and realized I had forgotten my cereal and was so upset I started to cry. I called my titi Priscilla, who didn't even drive, for sympathy. As expected, she said, "Stop crying. I'll take a cab; meet me downstairs." And she brought me my cereal and milk. Boy, was I a spoiled but happy girl. This went on for nine months! I would have Hanif running missions every day; Jamaican food, carrot juice... I ate anything I wanted–no controlled diet for me–and Hanif got it for me.

Throughout my pregnancy, Hanif never missed a doctor's appointment; my Papi was a dedicated man and would do anything to make me happy.

This was such a fun time for us. For the whole family, actually, since from the beginning we had been sharing our excitement. April of that year we finally got a bigger apartment, and fixed a room for our bundle of joy. I had always hoped for a baby boy who would looked just like Hanif. But Hanif said he would like a baby girl. Of course 'healthy' was our first concern. We were ready.

I had declared earlier that if we ever had a baby girl, I would name her Unique Cheron Lalloo. But now with a baby really on the way, my mom, my mother-in-law and Hanif all disagreed. They said "that's not a name." It took some time to convince me, but we all laid on my bed one day and came up with the name Monique instead of Unique. Well that was close, and it was an uncommon name back then, and it sounded beautiful, so Monique it was, and my family was relived.

I worked right up until my due date, October 18, and thought I would have the baby very soon. But after two weeks off work I was still home, waiting impatiently. I couldn't sleep at night anymore, and that made me crankier. I was sick and tired of everyone asking me, "Did you have the baby yet?" So I stopped answering the phone. For another week and a half I waited.

After a typical frenzied rush to the hospital late on November 10th, we waited again. Finally on November 11, 1985, at 3:27am, I delivered an 8 lb., 4 oz. baby girl named Monique Indira Lalloo and she had a very happy Papi and Mema. I was in labor seventeen hours; she was in no hurry to arrive. But her Papi never left my side. *(Thanks, Papi, we couldn't have done it without you!)* I had heard some women say that your spouse just got on your nerves when you were in labor, but I found the opposite to be true. I would have given up if it weren't for my Hanif's support.

That day the nurse came into my room and said, "You had twenty people here last night; you must be special!" Throughout my hours of labor it seemed like I was in a dream. Hanif would go in and out giving updates on my progress.

At one point I noticed a man coming in my room with scrubs on just like Hanif, but the closer he got the less he looked like my husband. As he got closer the eyes looked familiar... then I heard a voice say, "Sis, it's me, Michael." In pain, I laughed— my brother had talked my husband into the bathroom and exchanged clothes so that he could come in and see me! My brother does have a dry sense of humor, but this was the funniest thing he'd done!

Hanif had gone home to take a shower and get some rest. But Papi never really rested. It seemed like he was back in no time with two dozen red roses: one dozen for me, thanking me for having his baby, and one dozen for Monique with a card that said: *Your Papi loves you.* I saw in his eyes something I had never seen before. He had already fallen deeply in love with his baby girl. He really should have rested when he had the chance; we had no idea that we were soon going to be controlled 24/7. But this new bundle of joy brought more joy to the family than I'd seen in such a long time. And I was now starting in the hardest job I would take on—being a Mom.

As someone who felt it was important to bring 100% to the table, I had been expecting to step right into my role as Super-Mom. What an eye-opener it was, bringing home a tiny new life! I got my first taste of how children can break your spirit. My confident personality deserted me and I was frightened at the thought of being alone with sweet little Monique. I had to get used to breast-feeding; even that was overwhelming: how would I know when she'd had enough?? I would wake up to check that she was still breathing.

As always, Hanif stepped up to the plate. He woke up at night to take care of her. He would even pump my breast to store milk for the night so he didn't have to wake me—even though I was on maternity leave and he had to go to work in the morning. I found myself making believe I was sleeping so he would get up. At the beginning, Papi was a better mother than I.

Monique was a good baby, very peaceful right from the start. It wasn't long before I settled into motherhood, but her Papi was never far away. When she started eating, Hanif would puree all her food–*fresh!* Then he stored it for her to eat; she never ate store-bought baby food out of a jar. He surely earned his new title, "Mr. Mom." God had sent me a man who would be the best dad to my children. God is good...this I know!

For the next 3 months Monique and I spent a lot of time together and my fear gradually turned into calm and I was able to enjoy loving my daughter who I had wanted so badly. I was learning to enjoy the role of motherhood–a role to date I love and cherish the most.

By now, Monique had already become very close to her Papi. For the first couple of months, he gave her baths every day, fearing that I would drop her. I was feeling awkward and clumsy and I dropped everything, so the more he wanted to do, the more I let him do. He was the best dad my family had seen, and my mom was very pleased. She had been praying for this too. As years went on, we were a happy and loving family. Wherever Hanif was, Monique wasn't far behind. She was the type of baby that you could take anywhere she would never complain; she would go with the flow. Being the first daughter, granddaughter, and niece, the family couldn't get enough of her–she was a very special baby girl. She was nearly suffocated with love and affection.

Life was good, and then one day it got even better. Hanif obtained a contract, with the same management company where I had been working for the past few years, to do their ceramic tile work–for all 100 buildings! This was just the opportunity we needed to become financially comfortable.

We had all the materialistic things any young family can ask for. We'd been married just five years, Monique was two, and we were enjoying the finer things in life. We traveled a lot. We bought a lovely condo and we both had nice cars. We were happy, in love, we had money–what more could we ask for?

Monique was also living well. She was a bright child, and eager to learn, so we enrolled her in a Montessori school which she loved.

I stayed busy in my role as wife and mother, but I was now a less active daughter. Mom was now really suffering the depression of a lost life and marriage. She had started drinking vodka and orange juice from morning to night to mask her pain. It left her no chance to even try to improve her life. I was so used to having a strong woman for a mother; her attitude was frustrating and even made me bitter toward her. Naturally, I informed her that she wouldn't be able to spend time with Monique until she went for treatment. While that should have been incentive enough for her, it seemed she had no energy left to fight.

Finally the family knew they had to act or she would destroy herself, and we forced her into treatment. As Mom hit rock bottom, she finally agreed to work toward recovery; she was determined to have a relationship with her first granddaughter. The best gift she ever gave herself was one of therapy. A time to find out why she indulged her pain in the bottle. To think about finding herself. She had always been there for someone else–husband, children, sisters, brother, foster children–never for herself. This program was great; they had sessions in many areas of therapy teaching how to take control of life and bury pain behind. Soon she was well on her way to recovery, and looking forward to being the Mema (Grandma) she longed to be. We knew she had a long road in front of her, but without her addiction we would get through this together. I would never leave Mom's side. I needed her in my world and Monique needed her as well.

I was also blessed to have the best mother-in law who lived in the same building and was glad to help out whenever she could. Every day she came upstairs with new Jamaican remedies. One of them was olive oil from head to toe! Some remedies I wondered about, but I never questioned them aloud–I had much respect for Hanif's mom, and welcomed it all. On the other hand, Mr. Mom always had something to say, and anything that had to do with his daughter had to be approved by him. We women got such a kick out of his mothering–*nobody* knew better than he!

Other than my mom's problem, life was good. My mother-in-law moved to Florida so we spent some time going up and down the coast, always stopping at South of The Border–that was a must with Monique. Especially at night, she thought it was the coolest view in the world!

One day we decided to expand on our tile contract business, and we opened a store front in order to solicit additional work in private homes. We named the business after Monique: "M.I.L. Tiles." She used to say, "Papi, is this my store?" and he would say, "Yes Baby, everything Papi has is yours." The store had about nine employes–most of them family. I was one of them, which made it easier for me to be a full time mom and wife. The blessings coming my way were countless and I remained grateful. Our business ran smoothly for years.

But then the management company where I used to work ran into some problems that had to do with corporate politics. Their turmoil resulted in a slow down of our income. Getting to the top had come easy for us, but staying on top, and keeping what we had, was going to be a major challenge.

Money started to get tight, and our patience with each other ran on short fuses. It seemed Hanif and I fought about everything under the sun. He was turning 30 that year, and I believe he was going through a mid-life crisis. I knew there was something wrong besides our everyday squabbles. He became very short with me–something he had never done.

He is also a man of few words, and not quick to discuss his inner feelings. So it took time, but he finally laid it out for me. He said he thought we'd gotten married too young, and he needed some time to figure out what he wanted.

Wow, was I jolted! I never saw it coming. In a daze, I continued to work and live with Hanif; he didn't leave because Monique was very attached to him. How I suffered. I cried myself to sleep nearly every night since Hanif came in at any hour he pleased. On Sundays the three of us went out to keep some normalcy for the baby. Hanif was never mean or nasty to me; he just had a way of being cold. After a while, Hanif would sometimes stay out all night. Things started to get ugly between us. It was something I didn't know how to handle. Not a clue.

The prognosis for our marriage looked so bleak that it had me in a rage. One grey day I ended up balled up in my dark closet crying my eyes out and asking God to tell me what to do.

Hanif was the only man I'd known, and he had provided my comfort zone! Now the script was being rewritten and I was terrified of the unknown. I remember the day I forced myself to get a haircut, although I didn't feel much like getting spruced up. Once in the chair, the hairdresser started lifting my hair up and staring at my head. "What's wrong?" I asked. "You have several bald spots about the size of a quarter! Are you going through a lot of stress?" I just started crying, feeling so ashamed of how far my life had gone downhill. I told her to finish my cut, but then I needed to leave right away; wet head or no. Needless to say, I cried all the way home. And boy, did I let it out. That day I thought again about how I was the only one responsible for my happiness.

On a morning when Hanif had decided not to come home, we woke to a winter storm and we were snowed in–with no milk for the baby. Hanif would not answer his phone. I cried all day, and thought my heart would actually break...did people have heart attacks this way? The pain was so deep, and it had been that way for four months now. My mother wanted me to try to understand that these things happen with men. Sure, she knew from experience, but that didn't make it right. And anyway, it wasn't right to have it happen to *me*. That day I stopped trying to understand.

I asked Hanif to go out to dinner and talk about where we would go from there. "I don't want a divorce. I just need some time" he said. So we agreed to a separation, but without separating...because of Monique. A temporary "open marriage" is a better description. We'd stay living as we did, but I made it clear to him that I would not stay home any longer waiting on my husband to show up! I was going to go on with my life. Whenever he decided to return to me, then life would lead us, and until then Family Days would continue for Monique's sake, and he would take care of our lifestyle. He assured me he loved me and I assured him the same–only now, we had learned that love wasn't enough to hold us together.

The pressure was off, and believe it or not it felt a lot better. We were able to still make love–that remained the same. Hanif had by now closed our storefront, but he still kept busy and always took care of the bills–especially our daughter's needs.

During this time I started a job to put some extra money in my pocket, but also to keep busy–physically and mentally. For the next two years, I was a hard worker, and I learned to play hard. I began going out on weekends, staying out sometimes until 4 AM; something I had never experienced before and I liked it.

All my life, my outings had been with Hanif, with his family, or with my family. Since age 12, Hanif had been my focus. Now I realized that I needed to stand on my own two feet. I really didn't care what Hanif thought now; it was all about getting to know me. (Little did I know that would take a lifetime.)

It wasn't long before I discovered *me*. My newfound lifestyle was exciting, and it was fun! I had lost a lot of weight due to stress, and looked good. But more than that, I felt good inside. Hanif spent a lot of time with Monique. Those days, he was the one who didn't like it when I decided not to come home. I found out men can give it but they sure can't take it.

It wasn't long before I found out there was another woman. Not just another woman, but a woman named *Monique!* Even though I half expected it, my poor heart was broken. More pain. More rage.

Incredibly, this person had the nerve to call me *at my job* and tell me how she loved Hanif and planned to take care of him. She also thought it was important that I know she was not the first. The other girl she mentioned was a well known tramp.

I followed the typical path of a scorned woman and set out to pay him back. I'm not proud of the infidelity, but I needed to know what it was to share time and space with another man.

Still, I knew that wasn't enough. I had to let go and let Hanif find himself. I found out that men need to feel they still have the X factor with other women. Not that he hadn't already tested the waters, but I guess he wanted to jump in head first now and I wasn't planning to stop him. The question was: What price would our marriage pay?

That was my reality to face head on. Easier said than done, but I was determined. Break the cycle. Along the way I would learn from my journey! In my time apart from Hanif, I learned to love other things and be loved.

By this time, Hanif's family had all moved to Florida, and his Mom wasn't aware of our problems. He would take Monique to visit, and on his next trip south he told his mother what we were going through. My mother-in-law and I still had a wonderful relationship and she called me, to hear my side of the story. I gave her the whole picture. As usual, she was very understanding, but asked me to work on our marriage because Hanif and I had a special love. She told me that she loved me no matter what.

My mom would often keep Monique on weekends, to give us time to be free...let off steam...and hopefully reconnect. She knew what we were going through.

And Hanif's mother would fly to New York City and pick up Monique to take her on tour. Her second husband was a famous singer in a rock and roll group from the 50's. Monique did love the spotlight; at times she was the life of the party. She traveled all over the country with her grandparents. She was happy to perform in front of anyone...not shy at all, to this day.

I thank God for all the help we had with our daughter, making life's lessons a little easier for us as a family. Monique was getting older and I needed to make decisions about my life so that it wouldn't hurt my baby girl! She was our life. A healthy home was important for her; but right now I was having *so* much fun, and I didn't want my party to end.

It wasn't long after my mother-in-law called that my own mother and the rest of my family stepped in to ask "Where are you going from here?" "Do you want your marriage?" Mom told me to "Look at the whole picture; do you love him?" I said, "Yes. Very much." "Then stop the running around," she said. "Hanif is a good man who got off track. You have a little girl to think about, and you both have done damage. It's enough."

Days went on, and I thought to myself, "Sure, now that I'm having fun everyone wants to tell me it's time to get it together!" I had been on such roll, having a good time with my two best friends, Tina and April. What fun we had!

But I agreed that it was time to get serious and work on my marriage—if that was what I truly wanted. My love and attraction for Hanif had never died, so my answer was yes. Needless to say, I had backed way off on my personal goals over the past year.

I needed to dig deep for inner strength, and to put my goals back in perspective quickly. I began by returning one day to the same church we were married in. It was late, but the church was open and I entered to find only one other person inside. I lit a candle, asked for guidance, then I got on my knees and prayed. I would go down to our local beach to walk and think, or sit on the sand and gaze at the soothing water. One day on the beach I remembered a poem that I'd put on my wall as a teenager. *"If you love something let it go. If it is truly yours, it will come back. If it doesn't return it was never meant to be."* I felt the message speak directly to my heart, and I knew my answer. I was going to let go and see if my love would return to me.

One morning Hanif was very angry—not often his nature—so I asked him, "What's wrong with you?" He said, "You know what's wrong with me." But I had no idea. I knew I had come in the night before at a very late hour, but that had been the norm for us both. The baby was still sleeping, so I said we would talk later on, when we were alone.

That evening we met up and went for a ride. We ended up parking at a lake where we had often played as children. Hanif began by saying that we couldn't go on the way we had been, and that *I* needed to make a decision on our marriage. I bitterly replied, "Oh. Now you want our marriage. Did you fall back in love with me? I'm confused Hanif; now that I've moved on, you want me back!" It was difficult for me to open up to him again. We argued and cried and talked—for about four hours—while our family worried if we were killing each other! He said, "Look, I'm sorry. I do love you more than anything in this world and don't want to lose you." I looked at him and thought about all the years we had invested. I knew full well that I never really stopped loving him; my stomach still had butterflies every time he was around. My mother's words came to mind: He's a good man, but a human man who makes mistakes. Slow down; think of your future and don't let this bump in life detour you. You fought a long time for this love; if you believe in what you two have, then don't let it go." Hanif held my arm and asked me, "Is this what you want? Do you want our marriage?" He wanted an answer that night. Just like a man. My face swollen and my head pounding, more tears ran down my cheeks as I carefully considered his question.

My decision could hurt others. This time, it was important to do this for *me* ...and not for the fantasy of the white picket fence. We were digging down to find the truth. In order to forgive each other we had to be honest and trusting; that wasn't easy but we did it. There was no denying how much we missed each other. I was unsure how we would overcome our infidelities; could the power of forgiveness dull the pain of those memories? So much crossed my mind I was ready to explode, but Hanif still possessed a calmness that made me feel we had a fighting chance. But I needed him to understand that I had changed.

I told him I never stopped loving him and I was willing to give our love a second chance. But I wanted to be sure that we were reuniting because it was the best thing for each of us—not just for appearances, or to avoid the turbulence of divorce, or for the sake of our daughter...but for the right reasons. After all, I had observed my mom making that mistake and dooming herself to more misery living with my dad.

The family called once or twice, but to their surprise we were fine! We had survived what would turn out to be the worst. Now we would rebuild. Our whirlwind rise to financial success had indeed proven to be too much too soon.

I promised myself I would never again become less than 100% in control. Anything or anybody deciding to move on should not rock your foundation like mine had just been rocked.

---

*Life shrinks or expands in proportion to one's courage.*

~ Anaïs Nin ~

---

CHAPTER 6
## *Love Endures*

As always, our baby girl brought joy to our days and helped us forget the past. She was a comfort to both of us.

However, as the weeks passed, the phone calls to my job kept coming, dishing out further information that would make it more difficult for Hanif and I to overcome the past. Now that he had broken off his outside affairs, the women were livid and determined to hurt us by letting me know just how much Hanif had shared with them. I was hurt, yes, but angry more than anything–I wasn't about to hold it in and build up resentment. I released it right back at him. But Hanif just put his trash back in the can. He was dead set on moving us forward.

During that conversation by the lake, Hanif had asked me to move to Florida for a fresh start. He had plans: "We can build a house of our own with a pool for Monique." It sounded good, but I told him I'd have to think about it. All my family was near me where we currently lived. The thought of leaving my precious mom and family behind scared me.

By now we had uncovered many truths about each other. A huge lesson we learned was to agree to disagree. Life went on, and like the rest of the world, we took it one day at a time.

Hanif took Monique and I on weekend trips to the Jersey Shore and Atlantic City. We also frequently went south to where his family was, in hopes he could convince me to stay there in Florida. The beautiful houses were affordable and were built to your liking. A house with a pool, and a washer and dryer right in the house. No more lugging clothes down to the laundromat! It started looking better and better. Yet, I was still reluctant to move. I had no family there, and how could I possibly leave Mom behind? Port St. Lucie was the small town in Florida we visited. The road my mother-in-law lived on was a dirt road with only three houses on it and the area around was wooded. They had no street lights making it very dark compared to New York where the City never sleeps. I was frightened of the unknown. I wasn't ready yet.

One morning while I was dropping Monique off at school, her teacher called to me and asked if I was having a baby. I said, "No. Why?" It seems that, at sharing time with the class, Monique had shared that we were having a baby. When we got home, her Papi and I asked her why she made that up. She started crying and said she didn't want to be the only child... she wanted a brother or sister. So we told her we would ask God to send us a baby. She was so happy!

That July, we thought it was time for a little family fun–just the three of us. So we went to Virginia Beach for five wonderful days. We didn't talk about the past or the future; we merely enjoyed the present. And, even with Monique along, it turned out to be just the romantic setting we needed to rekindle our fire. I was reminded just how much I loved my Hanif. Virginia really is for lovers!

The summer weather was lovely, and love was in the air. Hanif would take us down to Manhattan in his Porsche to go shopping and eat lunch in the nicest cafés.

Weeks later, I found out I was having a baby that we had conceived on Virginia Beach. The whole family was excited for us, but most excited was Monique. When we told her, she leaned back against the wall and looked so pale we thought she might faint! She said, "God said it was OK!"

Right away, Monique wouldn't let me do anything. She would say, "No, Mommy. You can't do that. You're having a baby." I laughingly answered, "That doesn't mean I can't do things. I'm fine. This is only the beginning. Wait until Mommy's tummy gets big."

Laying in her room one night she asked me if she could name her baby sister and I said with no hesitation, "Sure my love. We had her for you, so that when Mom and Dad are long gone you would have a sister to love."

That year, we had also been looking after my little cousin, Angelique. She was headed down the wrong path and we wanted to do what we could to nurture her, so she spent almost all her time with us. She was a lot of help with Monique and happy to hear that we were being blessed soon with another angel in the spring.

For the next nine months Monique looked after me. She wanted to shower with me, wash my hair, and dry me off, she wanted to lotion me down and to put her ear next to my tummy to listen to her sissy move. She sang to her and talked to her all the time, asking, "Mom, does she hear me?" "Yes baby girl, she hears you. And when she's born she'll know your voice." The look on her face was priceless. She became even more bonded with us; we were very happy.

As the holidays approached, Hanif suggested, "Let's go to Florida for Christmas." This time Monique and I were both excited to go even though it would be the first holiday away from my family. So we left the cold behind for a hot and sunny Christmas in beautiful Florida, with me five months pregnant. We looked at model houses and for the first time my mind started to believe that I could make the change. You see, Hanif's grandma had bought us a piece of property so we just needed to make the decision to build. His grandma–may she rest in peace–was the cutest grandma who adored her grandson Hanif, and let me know that she loved me too. She always stood by our side, and we sure did love her. She is now an angel in Heaven–gone from us but never forgotten.

When we returned to New York, there was a serious snowstorm. For a while, we couldn't get out of the house, and our cars were snowed in. By the time we finally did get out, we needed things from the supermarket. Hanif didn't want me (with the baby on board) to go but, stubborn me insisted. And, wouldn't you know it? I ended up slipping on some ice and down I went. I laughed (as I habitually do at such moments). I wasn't hurt, but I had scared Hanif who didn't think it was funny at all.

That evening we were exhausted from the hustle and bustle in the snow. When Hanif said, "That's it; we're moving to Florida," I finally agreed. It was time to get away and make a change. We'd go as soon as our baby arrived and was old enough to travel.

Nevermind that I was ready to jump in the car and head to the hospital, my due date, March 18 sailed right on by. *Oh no, not again!* I was not a happy camper. Fifteen days later, on April 2, 1993, at 10:27 a.m., our second baby girl was born. Monique had already named her Jacqueline Elyse, and she weighed 7 lbs, 14 oz.

Hanif was the happiest man on earth, and I was the happiest woman. I often tease my Jacqui that she was made on the beach.

We were looking forward to our new family life in Florida.

———————

Love many, trust few, and
always paddle your own canoe.

———————

CHAPTER 7

## *Changing My Environment*

In June of 1993, we said our good-byes to my family and the town that held so many memories–the good the bad and the ugly. But it was time to make a change. Monique was 7, Jacqui was three months old, and I was broken-hearted leaving Mom behind. My dad was hurt because we had only recently started a relationship and now I was taking off. On the other hand, my mom encouraged me to spread my wings. I knew she would be just a phone call away but that didn't ease my heartache. My Titi Priscilla, as always, was willing to help me out with the move. We flew with the kids, and Hanif drove down to get started before we got there.

This was such a big change, but a very good move for our marriage. Hanif had landed a job prior to the move, so every day he went off to work while I stayed home to raise the kids.

We were only in Florida about three weeks when I got a call letting us know that one of our dearest friends had passed away. I just couldn't believe it! I got off the phone and couldn't stop crying, my heart hurt so much. He was fine young man who had come by the house before Hanif left for Florida. He made us laugh and gave Monique and Jacqui lots of love and kisses. Now his wife—my girlfriend—was left with two small children and a big hole in her heart. The two of them were supposed to follow us to Florida so we could raise our kids and grow old together. I couldn't get in touch with my girlfriend. I needed to be by her side to comfort her.

I didn't want to give Hanif such bad news at his new job, so I waited to tell him at the end of the day, but when he got home all I could do was to burst into tears. He finally calmed me down enough to deliver the tragic news. Hanif called his brothers and they came over right away and we made a plan. They were going to drive north and take Monique with them, and I would fly with Jacqui. It was the saddest goodbye I had experienced at that time.

Weeks later, we invited my girlfriend to come to Florida with the kids. When she arrived, I saw the lost look on her face and the darkness around her eyes. A part of her had died too. We made the best of the time; and the kids kept us busy. After they left I felt lonely. I missed my family a lot. The culture was different, I felt different, and I had no job. I knew I had to find a life.

My cousin Ann came down one summer, and we had such a ball that Hanif and I thought maybe she should stay. She could help us out with the kids, and in turn we would help her, and get her out of New York City! The pay scale in Florida was unbelievably low. There was no way I'd ever be able to work and pay someone to watch the girls.

Now strictly a stay-at-home mom, my resolve to keep myself 100% independent was being compromised. I thought if Ann stayed I could somehow be able to make a living and be a help to my husband.

One day as I was watching tv, a commercial for college turned on a light bulb in my head. I thought, "That's it! I need to go to college and find out what interests me." The very next day I went to talk to one of the counselors. She spent several hours with me going over different programs and looking up what I would qualify for in the financial aid department. We came up with a game plan. I leaned toward the medical field which offered a two year AS degree in science including a course in phlebotomy. This felt perfect for me.

I was so excited; I felt myself cracking the shell of my existence in order to emerge to a new level. That night when Hanif came home I told him I wanted to start school. As always, he was behind me. My only problem was how to juggle being a full-time student, and a mom, and a part-time worker at the job I was getting ready to find.

Days later I went to check out a preschool for Jacqui. And–*joy!*–the preschool I enrolled Jacqui in would take her for free part time, as long as I worked at least part time. So my plan was working out, and I couldn't have been any more pleased. Poor Jacqui wasn't too happy about going to school; she was a very shy baby and didn't want anyone but me.

So I did it; I started college to obtain a degree in science. I was very excited about this decision. I worked part time and went to school full time. The plan with Ann didn't quite work out, but my mom came down one Thanksgiving and I begged her to stay. Now she said if I found her a house she would come and help me with the girls if I was going to go to school. Of course we looked and found her a house–not 10 minutes from us!

Soon after, Mommy and her second husband Bebo moved into their new home. Bebo was another blessing to my family, and they were Heaven-sent grandparents. Their huge help with both of our girls allowed me to go to school for my degree.

The next two years weren't easy. I worked two part-time jobs, went to school full time, and was full-time mother and wife. I could once again truly appreciate my mom's talents, as I was now the one wearing many different hats. It seemed impossible some days, but then I reminded myself I had a lot of help. I had my mom, Bebo, a great helpful husband, and faith in my Heavenly Father who never let me down. If Mom could do it... well, with all my blessings, I could surely find a way!

Mom and my mother-in-law have been great examples in my life, and there have been many other strong women as well. I drew strength of each of them, to fit my needs.

In addition, I could see that my struggles to balance family and career were not unique. I was just one of millions of women in the same boat. Some days it felt like more than I could handle. Many a night during my college years, I struggled; often exhausted, sometimes in tears.

It was a long two years, but giving up was never an option! And then finally, Graduation! I was filled with a great sense of joy and accomplishment. I had been placed in the highest paying position of all those in my class. It was my most difficult, yet most satisfying achievement. Education is power!

I was placed in the field of oncology–radiation, to be specific. There I worked with a very nice and helpful doctor for the next five years. Fifteen years later, he is still a friend. It was hard work, but enjoyable too. Oncology is an amazing field. I faced an intense day-to-day struggle keeping my feelings under control. A happy atmosphere was important to our patients. I was able to make them feel loved and make them laugh– even though some of their lives would soon lose the battle to the scary disease of cancer. I was grateful I had entered this rewarding field of work.

After five wonderful years in that job, the doctor decided to move his office. It was too far away for me to commute, in case my children needed me in a hurry, so the doctor found me a job with a new physician in town who hadn't even opened his office doors yet. The new job was in the field of cardiology, where I've been for the past thirteen years. It is another medical field that I've grown to love and understand. This doctor has also been a blessing in many ways, but here I also learned about office politics and getting lost in the shuffle. Still, I always give all I have to our patients. It's been a hard road; one that I have learned to accept.

In the meantime, my mom was close, my husband was always working hard, my children were growing, and I was as happy as I could be. Other family took turns coming down to see us, which I loved. Titi Priscilla moved down, and soon I had a good bunch of my family living in Florida. I knew Hanif and I had made the right decision to relocate from New York.

Hanif and I both had decent jobs. Now we started thinking about building our dream home; a real "home," not a condo, or apartment. A place to bring our friends and family. So, we finally built a lovely house. It had a huge pool with hot tub area, which was yet another blessing. I always hated the community pool where I grew up. I was happy my girls wouldn't have to swim with strangers! And they would have their own rooms; every girl needs her own space. I know I did.

Hanif and I were thrilled with our new house, and life was grand. I was feeling *100% me*, and Hanif was happy, and together we were 200%. Now that's a healthy marriage! I was no longer afraid; I knew exactly who I was.

The largest part of me was still mom and wife. Being Mother was my most comfortable/most difficult role. I'd had a plan... We'd had a vision ... And here was the house with the pool, our two beautiful girls that meant the world to us, the doggy and the fish... And our house was a home.

As a child, I remember hearing adults say how time would fly by, and now I understood. Years passed, and Hanif and I showed the girls much love and a stable foundation. We worked hard, and hoped that our children would learn by watching.

Monique and Jacqui had a solid life. Their Papi and I made sure they needed for nothing, and they had more love and attention than most would see in a lifetime. Our days were filled with softball, volleyball, modeling, singing lessons, piano lessons. We kept Monique busy, and thereby kept ourselves busy chasing her around. We supported her every move; we were proud parents and Monique was a model child. The girls are seven and a half years apart, making things more special for them. They were able to experience the joys and agonies life throws at children at different times. And what a nice long break for Mom between the terrible twos! I often thank God for that age gap, or I would have had trouble coping.

---

*Raising a teenager is like trying to nail jello to a tree.*

---

CHAPTER 8

# *My Happy Heart Breaks*

That first year in the new house flew by. I constantly babied the girls–hoping to slow their childhood and delay the day they would have to face being an adult. We spoiled them rotten, but we also had a plan. The plan was: move them out of New York and into a slower lifestyle, give them more love than they could ask for, set aside college funds, and give them a solid foundation. We'd give them the tools and it would be up to them to use them. We had the perfect plan, and my children would follow *me* in breaking the cycle.

But now our girls were getting big. It was at this age that the girls didn't want to share things with Papi. At first I felt lucky, since up to now they had seemed more attached to their papi. I was a dedicated mom, but my devotion was constantly tested. As the girls matured, their lifestyles changed and it was time for me to learn to let go (well, that part I'm still working on). Our children need to learn how to fly, but they also need a lesson in how to fall and get back up. I tried to hold on to them because letting them hit the floor just didn't appeal to my maternal instincts.

Soon I was facing the high school years with Monique. I expected everything would be wonderful for my daughter, but life is what it is, not what you expect it to be. Somewhere around eleventh grade I started catching her in wrong doing.

When she got her driver's license, we bought her a car. Big mistake. 'Have car will travel!' and, get around she did. She kept friends we didn't approve of, and made some immature choices. Mostly it seemed like normal teenage rebellion, and she let it be known she couldn't wait to fly the coop: "Don't worry...I'll be out of here soon!" was a typical response to any disapproval we voiced.

The same year she graduated from high school, we had a family reunion in Hawaii. Great! What better therapeutic getaway? We would remove her from bad company and clear her mind. It was a fun and memorable trip, visiting with so many family members, and keeping busy. As always, I tried to make the best of family time, and Monique joined in most of the activities. But she stayed somber, and wanted to sleep a lot.

I thought everything would soon return to normal, but unfortunately she stayed depressed. We wanted her to stay nearby at a local college, but she was determined to go away to school. Not sure it was a good idea, we arranged some therapy for her, and it seemed to help, so we agreed to let her go. Actually, she was already 18 by then, and we thought that we really needed to let her go and test her wings. 18 or not, the day we took her to college and set her room up was harder than I thought it would be. As we walked away, I was heartsick.

It turned out college away wasn't a good choice for Monique, since she treated it as an opportunity as to go wild. Granted, most college students will let loose and have some fun while away on their own for the first time. But we hoped she would soon settle down and show us her responsible side. After two years we knew our girl hadn't been ready for that experience. Her grades were not improving enough to warrant us supporting her in a private apartment out of town. She would have to come home and attend the local college.

Naturally, living back at home didn't work for her, because at home we had guidelines. After those two years on her own she didn't like having to follow our rules. She rebelled by dropping out of local college and once again hanging out with the wrong crowd.

We realized that our plans for her future no longer mattered. Her future was in her own hands—for good or for bad, and our hopes for her were shattered.

Monique and I had been close just a short time ago, so it was painful for me to watch her run the opposite way. All her life I had been the best mom I could be; now I had no control to change her direction or to protect her. It broke my heart and her dad's—our whole family was hurting for her. The streets were stealing my daughter, and I was up for the fight of my life.

After a while people advised me to "Cut your ties with her, and let her hit rock bottom." I would cry and say, "Where is rock bottom?? That could be an unbearably bad place; I refused to let my firstborn go there!"

Moms are supposed to save their children, not let them go and watch them kill themselves. My mom never let me go and I wasn't about to let Monique go. I believe that children are a gift from God. So if they're weak and lost, should we allow the streets to eat them and spit them out? Not me. I couldn't sleep at night knowing that the streets had my child. I often had dreams of Monique screaming for me—asking me for help. But when I woke, I would confront her and she would say everything was fine. I couldn't find it in my heart to turn my back on God's gift to me. I let God know that I would forever treasure her, and I would not let Him down.

I also thank my Heavenly Father for the blessing of Jacqui. I had only wanted one child, but I was grateful for my second daughter. It was her youth and innocence that kept me in awe of motherhood; she kept me busy, and my days filled. Now, years later, I was off and running again, chasing after her to her big girl activities. Jacqui was a sensible child with a confident nature–a strong personality like her mom. We tried to shield her from all the darkness her big sister Monique brought to our lives, but I was later shocked to learn there were many things she knew about. For the past 18 years I had been raising–and lately just "dealing" with–Monique. I needed to give my maturing baby girl her time with me. She deserved a full mom, not a half.

I was the mother of two, but one was grown, and now it was time to let her go. It's a normal part of family life, but it was the hardest thing this mom ever had to do. I put her in God's hands. She was out of control, and breaking my heart. I tried to take one day at a time, but one day my heart just couldn't take anymore. I simply had to overcome the fear of letting her go. Finally the moment came that I had known was coming: in the heat of the moment I told her "If you don't like the rules in this house, there is the door!" To my surprise, the next day she moved out of our home and in with her college roommate…not the wisest decision, but she wasn't making many wise decisions at the time. I had finally let go.

Later, I looked back and counted myself grateful for those first 17 years Monique gave us, when she was a good child and never any trouble. She just went with the flow. Maybe that was the problem… going along with others, not analyzing where she was and what she was doing. The flow swept her away from us. My heart was gray, and those were rough years for our family, but our faith held us together.

Jacqui, in her teens, was strong-willed in thought and mind, and she had the ability to see life clearly. She even picked me up several times when I was down and made me face facts: how I needed to leave Monique alone, and let her live her own life. It was my baby girl that saved my soul. With a good husband by my side, my baby girl, family, and my faith, I would be fine.

I reclaimed and nursed my soul, reinforcing it to withstand future devastation. Life wasn't stopping because of my problems, so I got my mind, body and soul in alignment and moved on with the rest of the world. I was a mother of two, not one, and I would not let anymore time pass while my second gift from God patiently waited. I would not let her down.

It took me a long time to realize that I only gave two gifts to my girls. First was the gift of birth. From that moment on, *they* would build who they were. My views were just that—*my* views. Seasons change, and reasons change, and kids grow up to be whoever they are! I needed to not take that personally. It was a challenge, but I learned to accept it.

The second gift I've given them is my unconditional love. Experience taught me the definition of "unconditional." My adoration and devotion for my family was enduring, in a real world that was nothing like I had envisioned it to be.

## Reflections of a Mother
### AUTHOR UNKNOWN

I gave you life, but cannot live it for you.
I can teach you things, but I cannot make you learn.
I can give you direction, but I cannot be there to lead you.
I can allow you freedom, but I cannot account for it.
I can take you to church, but cannot make you believe.
I can teach you right from wrong, but cannot always decide for you.
I can buy you beautiful cloths, but cannot make you beautiful inside.
I can offer you advice, but I cannot accept it for you.
I can give you love, but I cannot force it upon you.
I can teach you to share, but I cannot make you unselfish.
I can teach you to repect, but I cannot force you to show honor.
I can advise you about friends, but cannot choose them for you.
I can advise you about sex, but I cannot keep you pure.
I can tell you the facts of life, but I can't build your reputation.
I can tell you about drinking but, I cannot say "NO" for you.
I can warn you about drugs but I cannot prevent you from using them.
I can tell you about goals, but I cannot achieve them for you
I can teach you about kindness, but I can't force you to be gracious.
I can love you as a child, but I cannot place you in God's family.
I can pray for you, but I cannot make you walk with God.
I can teach you how to live, but I cannot give you eternal life.
I can love you with unconditional love all of my life....
    And I will!!!

    Love always, Mom

CHAPTER 9

# *What Happened? / Losing Control*

*"Marriage & Motherhood"* –It's the name of a roller coaster I've been riding for years; some days wondering if the safety bar would fail, and I would fly out screaming!

When my children were not on the right track, I felt off track too. I had lost my Monique, and discovered the void left by an absent child simply cannot be filled. Watching her go left me hurt and bewildered. I struggled to process the information in front of me, and eventually concluded: No matter what a parent does and what tools they give their children, it's only what those children do, and how they use those tools that can shape their lives. My girls would have to make their own mistakes and there was nothing I could do but pick them up when they fell, wipe them off, and send them on their way.

I always tried to give 100%, but knowing that I didn't always get the same in return was hard. Still, throughout the years I vowed to do my best, and to keep the faith. So many times I kept my inner pain hidden. Because, I was the mom and I knew that moms never break down. In order to keep a somewhat normal life, I had to keep my cool and keep my family together. That's what women do.

There were days I asked myself, "Where do I come in? *WHAT ABOUT ME?*" Mom always told me that my Heavenly Father wouldn't give me more than I could handle, but…

My constant battle to keep it together was some days more than I could handle. I began to look forward to my 20-minute drive to and from work, relishing the privacy it granted me. That was where I cried till I had no more tears, and could finally put life back in perspective. I'd wipe my tears, and then put on one of the many hats I had to wear. Mom was right; I couldn't understand until I was there myself. I tried to wear them well.

One reason I had trouble along my way is that I am an all-or-nothing personality type. But when you're raising children, life isn't so easy to sort out. It's hardly ever black or white; but lots of grey! In order to survive I had to adjust my stand of always operating at 100%. Soon it became 50% and sometimes lower, and I was sad to see *my children* were the ones holding me back!

My (once) crucially important priority list flew out the window. Personal plans dropped down into the "if there's ever time…" column; and I made sure I took care of our girls and was a good wife and housekeeper. Exactly how I was brought up. The rewarding job of motherhood that I had yearned for? I was learning it was the hardest job in the world, *and* there was no "happily ever after" in sight.

I asked God the age-old question: Would He teach *me* to understand the things I could not change and the wisdom to know the difference?

I have always been a dreamer. Constantly visualizing my life and how I thought it would be. Maybe I was born dreaming!

As a child, I visualized having a better life. I had decided then, if I planned out my life and I gave my children a loving dad, they would not need to search for love in all the wrong places.

As a woman, with one child grown and another going through her formative teenage years, it became painfully apparent to me that keeping control of the people and events in your life is not that easy. Doing all that you can think to do does not always suffice. My heart had been broken, and I was forced to face the fact that, in love and life, there are no guarantees.

If I was going to save *myself* somehow through all that I found myself facing, I would have to fight. Good thing I am a fighter, and I knew I could survive a battle.

I remembered how staying too long in a bad place makes it harder to break away. Also how some of the women from my past never made it.

---

### Living through Music

You know blessed be the Lord my strength,
Which teaches my hands to roar and my fingers to fight.
Through it all He's protected me along the way.
And I wanna thank you.
'Cuz without you I'm nothing.
I know it gets a li'l hard, but He will take care of you.
If you trust and believe and have faith.

from: "Just Like You" –Keyshia Cole

---

Ever feel like you're
different from the rest of the world?

That's God's gift to us,
like footprints and finger prints.

You're not different...
you're unique!

CHAPTER 10

# *It Began to Change Me*

I started this book at 40. That's when I finally let go of the things I had no control over. And the truth is, the *only* control I had was over myself.

During our struggle to guide our first daughter, the extended family went through a heart-rending experience. My niece Jessy, only 17, suddenly passed away from a congenital heart defect that nobody was aware she'd had. It hit me hard—Jessy and Monique were about the same age! Grief over Jessy's death, and thinking about her parents' staggering loss brought my heart to a new level of pain. After that, throughout the hard times, my sister-in-law–Jessy's mother–always reminded me to "Thank God you still have your children."

I thought a lot about our time on this earth. Most of us assume our lifetime is a span of eighty- or ninety-something years. *But there is no such promise!* We should be living each day as though it were our last, and making time to love ourselves as well as others.

By now I'd spent a lot of days praying The Serenity Prayer. It's ironic; I grew up thinking it was for the weak and the addicts of the world. Now I'm a firm believer that we are all just a step away from weak, and our addictions are many.

> *"God grant me the serenity to accept the things I cannot change; courage to change the things I can; and wisdom to know the difference ..."* —Reinhold Niebuhr

It had been a long four-year strained relationship with Monique until she moved out at 20 to start a life of her own. But now I accepted that both my babies would make their own decisions. Decisions their father and I may not agree with. I prayed Monique would make hers wisely. She was already on her journey, so I became a 'standby mom;' if she needed me she'd call, but I was no longer in control of her life.

Anyway... I had other work to do. I had another girl who still needed my attention. And I had myself to minister to; where had my "self" been hiding? I had prayed for help, and now it was time to change the things I could change. I wanted to fulfill all the roles in my life to be best of my abilities: daughter, mother, wife, and myself.

First I worked to take care and nurture my own needs; I was a person too and if Mommy wasn't happy, nobody was happy. Taking control of myself wasn't always easy; it could put a wedge between me and the ones I love. But I had to take the chance and step out.

I had turned 40 in the midst of turmoil. But, reflecting on the mature age I had reached and what I had managed to achieve in my life up to that day was quite enlightening. It gave my spirit a much needed lift and made moving on easier; I finally put myself back up at the top my list.

Life had taught me to take a punch.

My early vision of a perfect life was swept away, but it didn't matter. As a family, we accepted the changes and grew from them. We had another teenager to raise and I was eager to do so; no longer afraid of reality.

I had felt like a jigsaw puzzle, pieces scattered; but I'd picked them all up and put together a beautiful picture of... *me*.

I learned to concentrate on positive energy; and to appreciate my many blessings.

I forced myself to stop carrying others' luggage and to worry only about keeping my own as light as possible.

I strove to be a woman who would make my parents proud; a woman who shared a legacy of change and who cared about breaking the cycle.

I had another passion for journaling. Writing always made me feel better and my soul feel lighter. I always kept pencil and paper nearby and whenever I was alone would record my feelings.

I began to walk three times a week — about two miles a day. Before I knew it, I was running those six miles a week. With my mind clear and music in my ears, it was me against the world. My mind, body, and soul felt aligned for the first time in years. I started to like the woman in the mirror. I felt whole.

I participate in different foundations... one is the Pajama Program which gives new pajamas to children in the State's care. Another is collecting prom gowns for inner city youth.

And the one especially near and dear to my heart is the Jessica Clinton Foundation, established by my sister-in-law Cheryl whose pain over the loss of her 17 year old daughter motivated her to save others' lives. The Foundation raises money for defibrillators for schools in St. Lucie and surrounding counties. These are things that define me and it is my belief that most of the blessings I'm receiving are from giving back to our youth—where my heart has always been.

I have mentored many teenagers; both young ladies and young men. Being a mother of two girls, my home stays filled with young people. I spend a lot of time with them in hopes that if even one hears and heeds me, then I've given back some of my blessings. Children *are* our future. It's not just a song lyric. I'm letting them know that they can be a part of breaking the cycle.

I want to leave behind a lifetime of giving to the young girls of the world not only my girls. I want them to know that it is ok to be happy and that it doesn't always include others' happiness. I want them to know that education is a power no one can take from you and that life is not about living behind a white picket fence but about building that fence.

I started making choices just for me. I had always wanted a breast reduction. I even wanted tattoos! I picked out a new car just for me. Occasionally I would travel with my girlfriends. Sometimes my views were not the same as my husband's and family, so I didn't always make everyone happy, but I needed to be me.

Even with all my blessings, there are still so many things on my list left for me to do. I have a voice inside always asking to experience more. I say, "If you believe it, and you can see it—whatever it is—it's in your reach. Don't let anyone tell you your dreams aren't reachable."

I'm proud of staying true to me when being me wasn't always easy.

God made women strong. We bear the children, and experience the good, the bad, and the wonderful miracle of it. We devote ourselves to our children, putting them before our own needs and desires, yet sometimes we face rejection from those that we nurtured. Still we keep going. We dare not give up.

For me, I owe my strength to my beliefs. I am a woman of deep faith which gives me perseverance. I gave my family everything I had from an early age, and then I reached a crossroads. Of course I'm not the picture of perfection, but I know the best gift I can give my daughters is to lead by example. I want to leave behind a life that I can take responsibility and credit for. My Journey. A legacy that I'm proud of.

I now know that my gift to me is taking care of my soul for the rest of my life. I have made many changes…I decided to stop trying to save the world, and instead just change myself. That will contribute to the world. I have put myself on The List, making sure I am happy so that I can give back.

I am woman. Simple, yet complex. I love deep and wear my heart on my sleeve. I have many passions in life, and one is recording my hopes and dreams. I love music, laughing, traveling, and observing the various ways other people experience life.

At 46, I am comfortable in my body. I can easily ignore any nagging images from the past of the perfect shape I used to be. It's OK to let go of the perfect image.

I am always ready to learn more about myself. At the end of the day, I will be able to live, love and laugh knowing I've done the best with ME.

———————

Be the kind of woman who
when your feet
hit the floor each morning
the devil says,
"Oh Crap, She's up!"

———————

CHAPTER 11

# *Breaking the Cycle*

To break my habits, I turned to my Heavenly Father. I asked for guidance, for strength to not question His plan for me, and to keep me on the right path. My faith grew stronger, and it became easier to follow.

I had become a woman of substance. I am wiser. I cry. I laugh. But I learned in Whose hands my power lies, and together we can weather any storm.

Time after time, I thanked God for the husband He sent to me. So many years went by when I felt nothing was more important than my children. I was so intent on mothering I didn't realize I was leaving him behind. But that man never gave up on me. Hanif never turned his back on the woman he married, nor on the woman she later became. My husband – even though he didn't always understand and agree with my mothering ways and my decisions – always supported me. He is a steady man of quiet strength, and he taught me that sometimes silence speaks loudest.

I'd had other sturdy safety nets too. My loving aunts. My mother, one of the most loving women I know, always gave me reality checks. She was always standing by—with her love and loyalty to both my girls a constant blessing.

All along the way, I found good examples: other women who opened my eyes to different perspectives of life. I hope that I can also lead by example and that my life helps other young girls.

There are many common sense steps to take in life that will keep us from taking the wrong path, but never forget that the Man above has a custom plan for each of us, and if we don't listen, we will never discover it.

I believe my dream of breaking the cycle was part of His plan for me. I was led to be aware of my path while still a child watching women in my life. I vowed to make my life different, and I did.

In my journey thus far, taking forty-plus years, I have held fast to my vow that no man would ever determine my self worth; and in fact I would not allow *anyone* to determine that but the Lord above. **This is the key I hold.**

I hope you can find your key much sooner than I did. Start with a plan and keep in mind that life will try to throw you off course. Love yourself first and own who you are.

Chapter 12

## *Parting Words*

I have loved and been loved. What a wondrous and intoxicating emotion! And powerful! So much so that at times it's necessary to control the depth of love. *Feelings* can overpower common sense in the blink of an eye, so remember to hold your heartstrings in check until you are sure that you are channeling your love to the right recipient. You should have a plan. You should be 100% in control of yourself–keep one eye on your path–and never to let the one you love pull you off-course.

I've been in love with my first love for thirty plus years and our journey has made us stronger. We have created two very special girls who I call my heart and my soul and as long as God grants me time on earth I will be their biggest fan.

I want my girls–no, *all* girls–to comprehend that not a single medal will be passed out for being a good mother or wife. That's why our initial goal must be self-fulfillment. Then we can truly enjoy filling the special pockets sewn into our hearts for husband and child. I hope all women will get to know who they really are–dig deep, at a young age, and discover the person within.

I am still a work in progress,
but after finding the key
to breaking the cycle,
I had to share
my walk in
the sand.

Normal day, let me be aware
of the treasure you are.
Let me not pass you by in quest of some
rare and perfect tomorrow.

~ Mary Jean Irion ~

*How I Broke the Cycle...*

# Special *Thank You's*

### To My Heavenly Father

*A very special thanks.
I feel You carrying me each and every day.
I am trying to listen, and to follow Your lead. Although
I am not perfect, my love for You will always be.
At the end of my journey, You will be the only One who matters.
I'll see You on my judgement day. All my love.....*

### To My Mom

*Your determination to survive without a mom taught me to count my blessings. You taught me to believe in the power of prayer and that faith is the key to my soul. You told me there was a lot I wouldn't fully understand until I became a mom. You were so right. You believed in me and my dreams.*  *As a supportive mother, you went beyond my expectations. Thank you for all the times you felt my pain and cried with me. Thank you for being a woman of worth. Last, but not least, thank you for keeping me when your plate was overflowing. I have been blessed with a mother who is an amazing lady to have in my corner. It is a privillage to call you my mom.*

### To My Brother

*Thank you for showing me that hard work pays off. Things may not always go as we plan, but you always reached for the top. Thank you for leading by example.
Love you bro; I will always be just a phone call away – oxoxo*

### *To My "Papi"*

*You have been the key to my happiness, and you will always hold the key to my heart. You were my first love, the first man to show me that special love that comes once in a lifetime, and you were sent from Heaven. Ours has been a 30-year romance that I wouldn't change for anything. Together we built a wonderful relationship on pure love. Thank you for being my soul mate; for allowing me to be who I am. Thank you for being an exceptional husband, son, son-in-law, and most of all a father to our girls. This blessing means the world to me. These are the KEYS to an everlasting love. Thanks for feeding my soul.*

## LOVERS AND FRIENDS

My companion throughout the good times and bad;
My friend, my buddy, through happy and sad.
Beside me you stand.

You'll talk, you'll listen to my pain and tears.
I know you'll be there throughout all my years,
If I should fall.

*And I'm so grateful! oxoxoxo*

## To My Dad:

Your strength is a blessing that I inherited from you. It has come in handy through some trying years. I thank God he gave us a second chance at rekindling our love. I discovered that you were a product of your environment and could only show me the love you were shown. I am happy to have had the opportunity to understand you and to get to know the man who gave me my that inner strength. I love the good in you that many never got to see. I'll always love you. —your only daughter, who fought you all the way! Sorry, Dad, but someone had to do it!!! I love you. oxoxo

**Titi Lucy, Titi Nancy, Titi Priscilla,** — You have given me inspiration. Watching you three, I was able to see first-hand what can be accomplished whether or not you're given any choices in

life. You had the gumption to improve on the lives you were dealt. You all made it work. And this young girl was there to learn – from your struggles – how to escape from a place I did not want to be. You have given me life lessons; the courage to fight, and to have faith in what I can't always see. You taught me that no man could ever take me to places I didn't choose to go! You protected me on all those stormy days. You spoiled me rotten, and eased my pain so many times. From the bottom of my soul, thank you for never leaving my side. You have all played a big part in the woman I am today. I hope I have made you all proud. Much love!

### To My "Girls" aka My Best Friends Tina & April

*Your struggles and perseverence have shown me that there is always hope. You each had a load of trials that not all women could have fought through as you both did. And it dared me to complain about mine. You are both so different, but your common ground is our friendship.*
*Thank you both... For always alowing me to be me. For all the laughing we've done—to the point where we couldn't breathe. And even for the crying we've shared; it made us stronger women.*
*I'll always by your side... girls to the end...oxoxo*

### To My Cousin Angilique

*You are the sister I always wanted.*
*You are a special soulmate.*
*I try to be an example for you, and I pray you will learn from others like me. Please help me break the cycle for women in our family.*
*Please believe in You.*
*Take one day at a time, and in that day, never forget your faith.*
*I will always be here for you. Love you toooo much.*

### To My Mother-in-Law, Veta

*Thank you for believing—when not many did— in the young love I had for your son. Your inner strength motivates me. Thank you for raising such a fine man— the love of my life.*

### To All the Strong and Motivating Women in my life

*In my life I have been blessed with many strong women who I have been able to use as guidelines.*

### To My Daughters

*This book is dedicated to you,
because you are both my heart and soul.
The best gift you can give Mommy is to
be the best that you both can be.*

### To Me, Myself, and I

*I want to remember and treasure every experience in my life.
Whether happy or unpleasant, each event was
a necessary 'step up' to reach the next level.
I am grateful for the depth of passion I've allowed myself
to reach, because it is the fire that lights my soul.*